David Shields
Scott Kent Jones

A CHRISTIAN EXISTENTIALIST AND A PSYCHOANALYTIC ATHEIST WALK INTO A TRUMP RALLY...

sublation press

A Christian Existentialist and a Psychoanalytic Atheist Walk into a Trump Rally…

First Published by Sublation Media 2024
Copyright © 2024 David Shields and Scott Kent Jones

All Rights Reserved
Commissioned and Edited by Douglas Lain
Copy Editor: Konrad Jandavs

A Sublation Press Book
Published by Sublation Media LLC

Distributed by Ingramspark

www.sublationmedia.com

Print ISBN: 979-8-9901591-7-4
eBook ISBN: 979-8-9901591-5-0

Edited and typeset by Polifolia in Germany

Praise for David Shields's *Nobody Hates Trump More Than Trump: An Intervention* (2018)

"I wasn't going to read it, because I was so tired of anti-Trump shit, but I love the book, agree with everything Shields nails about the moment. It's the best summation of Trump I've come across. Such a relief to see someone get it. I was reading passages to my millennial Communist 'Trump is going to kill us all' bf, who didn't say anything, just rolled away."

—Bret Easton Ellis, author of *American Psycho*

"Shields has the widest range of curiosity of any American writer I'm aware of, and he almost never wastes your time. He nails what's off-kilter and crazy about Donald Trump and the political psychosis he represents at least a hundred times, and in dozens of insightful ways. Shields is good enough, in this book, to earn the designation of being the writer most likely to be picked up and murdered should either right- or left-wing fundamentalists take power in the United States. This is a designation that hasn't been conferred on an American writer since Philip K. Dick. What I'm saying is that Shields is *that* good. He is one of a very small group of true 21st century writers worthy of the tag, and I salute him as a master."

—Brian Fawcett, *Dooney's Cafe*

"You're unlikely to encounter another book so recklessly and unpredictably full of insight, even wisdom. Shields is the most exciting writer we have in America at the moment, the most startling and innovative."

—Jeff Simon, *Buffalo News*

"Often brilliant."

—Toby Lichtig, (London) *Times Literary Supplement*

"A fantastic read."

Favorite Books of 2018
—Timothy Denevi, *LitHub*

"A sobering, nuanced, and—at times—brutally funny—psychological investigation into why Trump resonates with all, even the people who hate him."

—Moshe Schulman, *The Rumpus*

"A mesmerizing study of power, how it isolates, how it infantilizes, how it amplifies our collective fears."

—Cathy Alter, *Washington* [D.C.] *Independent Review*

"A compelling book offering something to offend nearly anyone."

—*Kirkus Reviews*

"Shields weaves together wry observations."

—*Publishers Weekly*

Favorite Books of 2018

—Neal Thompson, *Spokane Spokesman-Review*

"Shields's short book delivers the goods."

—Shannon Laster, *Open Letters Review*

"*Nobody Hates Trump More Than Trump* has something new to say."
—Neal McNamara, *Patch*

This is a detective story.

*

David Shields: What degree and angle of self-loathing necessitate Trump's obsession with being liked (not just liked but, rather, loved; not even loved but adored, worshipped) on a second-by-second basis? What sadness animates this need to be flattered and fluffed?

Francis Wilkinson says that Trump has "a titanic ego that is paper-thin," which is hardly a revelation, but the degree of thinness is what I find so fascinating. The clues are everywhere: his tyrannical father, his anhedonic mother, his obsessions with shit and piss and germs and death and being spanked (forcing Stormy Daniels to watch three straight hours of *Shark Week* with him when he's terrified of sharks: at last, a woman to simultaneously comfort him, as his mother never did, and judge and punish him, as his father always did).

*

Trump childhood friend: "He did talk about his father—how he told him to be a 'king,' to be a 'killer.' He didn't tell me what his mother's advice was. He didn't say anything about her. Not a word."

*

Shields: According to Peter Lovenheim, who for several years has been researching and writing a book about attachment theory, "The biographical record is fairly strong on Trump's failure to develop a healthy emotional attachment to either of his parents. Mary Trump became seriously ill from complications during labor with her last child, Robert. As a result, at just two years and two months of age, Donald endured the trauma of the prolonged absence and life-threatening illness of his mother. It's not clear how long she was incapacitated. Indeed, we don't know that she ever really re-engaged with her son.

"Friends of the Trump family who knew the Trump kids when they were young report that they 'rarely saw Mrs. Trump' and that Donald, while 'in awe' of his father, was 'very detached from his mother.' Much of the president's behavior is clearly consistent with attachment avoidance: his powerful sense of self-reliance and near inability to acknowledge self-doubt; his bragging about his sexual relations; his almost complete lack of friends; and his unstable relationships with White House staff, cabinet members, and congressional leaders of both parties. Overt narcissism or grandiose self-regard is associated with attachment avoidance."

This psychobabble is all pretty reductive, and yet there is a gigantic ghost in his machine, is there not? What is it? What "explains" him? Is he inexplicable? Is there such thing as pure evil? If so, what value is there in declaring it "pure evil"? None, in my view.

*

Childhood friend re Trump's mother: "She just did not interact with the kids when their friends were around."

*

Scott Kent Jones: In many ways, he just seems like the saddest person on the planet. And I think that's the secret to his connection with people.

Jones: You can't underestimate the intensity of Trump's obsession with movies and movie stars. When Trump was in high school, he desperately wanted to become a movie producer but was prevented from doing so by his father, who mandated that Trump enter the real estate business. Trump has been quite explicit in saying, *I've turned the real estate business into a subset of the dream factory.* What is Trump Tower but a kind of Disney ride?

*

Shields: At Trump Tower and Mar-a-Lago, Trump receives two scoops of vanilla ice cream with his chocolate cream pie, while everyone else at the table receives one.

*

Shields: At age seven he allegedly punched his elementary school music teacher, giving him a black eye, "because I didn't think he knew anything about music and I almost got expelled" (music teacher, who nevertheless refutes that Trump ever hit him: "Even then, he was a little shit").

*

Childhood neighbor re Trump: "He was known to be a bully. A loudmouth bully."

*

Shields: According to Trump biographer Michael D'Antonio, Fred's decision to send Trump to military school was "a very severe response to a kid who hadn't gotten arrested and wasn't involved in drinking and drugging. This was a profound rejection of Donald."

*

Shields: At New York Military Academy, he won a medal for "neatness." His roommate, who nicknamed him "Mr. Meticulous," said Trump folded his towels and underwear "so that every single one was perfectly squared—like, insanely neat."

*

Shields: Steve Hassan says that cult leaders tend to "have a feeling of insecure attachment to their mother and father. For their entire lives, they're compensating for that lack of sense of self by getting praise and kudos from the outside world. In Trump's case, he was raised in the church of Norman Vincent Peale, where doubt was considered evil."

*

A family friend on Fred and Donald: "It was very strange to see the two of them together in the same room. They were both talking, supposedly to each other, but neither heard what the other was saying. They talked right past each other."

*

Shields: The degree of Trump's obsession with Putin's interference illegitimatizing his presidency is in direct proportion to his knowledge that Fred's business success renders his son's "accomplishments" imaginary.

*

Shields: The media are his mother and father, from which and from whom he's forever trying to obtain complete and perfect love (good luck with that).

*

Shields: Among many other things Trump has learned from Howard Stern, he's learned to take himself down a peg or even several pegs, in a trivial way, before someone else does so in a more substantive way. For instance, *I'm building this incredible ballroom at Mar-a-Lago, one of the better things I've ever built and, you know, the first thing always is the marriage, but it* [his wedding to Melania] *is also a way of highlighting the ballroom.*

*

Jones: A Dostoevsky quote I find myself coming back to again and again: "What is hell? I maintain that it is the suffering of being unable to love." And it's pretty easy to get to Trump from here. When Stern asked, "Do you know what love is? Do you love anyone?" Trump couldn't answer. He just said something like, *I love Melania; she's hot.* He clearly had no access to love, and it was kind of heartbreaking.

*

Shields: "It's a Trump thing," Don Jr. says. "We have to end up winning. It's a fact of life."

*

Jones: Every Trump business venture has gone bankrupt. Nearly without exception. If he had simply allowed the hundreds of millions of dollars he inherited simply to accrue interest, he'd be far wealthier than he is now.

*

Shields: His father treated him as an employee. His mother treated him as an inconvenience. He was formatted from an early age to loathe himself.

*

Jones: I once heard someone say, "The first thing I saw when I came to New York was someone being mean to somebody else, so I just adopted that personality."

*

Shields: The Trumps owned thousands of apartments, some of them in the lower-middle-class, blue-collar Queens of the '50s, '60s, and '70s. A friend of mine who grew up in and around these apartments in Queens says it's important not to underestimate how much Trump's political rhetoric derives from his experience in these housing projects; Trump could see how many white, lower-middle-class, blue-collar people resented what they saw as government overregulation, getting pushed out by bureaucracy, certain parts of an apartment complex having to be reserved for Black occupants, "Black crime," etc. According to my friend, Trump learned how to build a politics of resentment—symbolic resentment—as the quasi-enforcer of the Fred Trump properties.

*

Shields: Nicholas Montemarano, who was born in Brooklyn, raised in Queens, and has written a *roman à clef* about John Edwards, says, "Most of the bullies I encountered growing up in Queens were of the Trump variety: their words were often worse than anything they actually did. They postured; they threatened; they demeaned. Many were tough, but what mattered more was that they seemed tough. Trump's policies and public persona, his crass statements and bullying demeanor, must certainly betray who he is—but only part of who he is. The storyteller in me can't believe that what we see and hear is all there is to Donald Trump. At times, he seems not to have an inner life. This is a man who doesn't even ask forgiveness from the God he pretends to believe in. I can't imagine him shedding a tear. And for all these reasons, I'm that much more compelled by him." Exactly. His emptiness is galvanizing.

*

Jones: If Trump were from, say, southern California, he'd be understood to be an LA narcissist; if he were from Chicago, he'd be understood to be a gear in a corrupt political machine. If he were (originally) from Florida, he'd be understood to be the emblem of that particular species of swampland insanity. Trump is a rather crystalline product of New York; in so many ways New York City created him, and he got away with murder there for decades.

*

Shields: Abe Wallach, a long-time Trump aide, told Tim O'Brien that if Trump "thinks you've got good genes," he'll do business with you.

*

Shields: *Should I say "figure" instead of "body"? It's a little more respectful. No, her body is amazing.* It's crucial to refer to the polite choice and the rude choice and then double-down on the rude choice. The (very mild) frisson is in the emptying out of politesse.

*

Shields: A friend, whose father worked in the CIA, cheats on his girlfriend because he doesn't feel alive unless he's being deceptive.

*

Shields: According to a source of Mika Brzezinski's, Trump's biggest complaint about life in the White House was that he was blocked from watching porn.

*

Shields: Is sexual obsession of this kind and to this degree ever not derived from early damage?

*

Shields: His supposed obsession, even in his 70s, with sex: this may be a mirage—both to himself and to the paying public. It's the one thing to or about him that seems even vaguely real. A lot of men feel this way: athletes, businessmen.

*

Ballet adage: "If it doesn't hurt, you're doing it wrong."

*

Shields: Whenever politicians whom I don't recognize show up on TV, I can immediately predict—based on how well-coiffed they are—with which party (and exactly which wing of that party) they're affiliated.

*

Shields: The dialectic of American politics is relentlessly schizophrenic: Eisenhower led to Kennedy; Nixon to Carter; Carter to Reagan; Clinton to Bush; Bush to Obama; Obama to Trump; Trump to post-Weinstein reckoning/purge; and now Biden back to Trump?

*

Stormy D: "I asked him about his hair. I was like, 'Dude, what's up with that?' and he said, 'You know, everybody wants to give me a makeover, and I've been offered all this money and all these free treatments.' And I was like, 'What's the deal? Don't you want to upgrade that? Come on, man.' He said that he thought if he cut his hair or changed it, he would lose his power and his wealth."

*

Shields: At cabinet meetings, Trump sat, Pasha-style, with his hands resting above his big belly.

Shields: At Davos, Trump sat on a white chair in exactly the same manner he sat on a white chair at his first press avail with Obama at the White House. His posture was for shit, his legs were splayed—his feet pointed in opposite directions—he was pouting/grimacing in that stereotypically 12-year-old boy way of his, and his hands were placed at the end of his tie, directly over his crotch and forming the exact shape of a uterus.

*

Shields: There is no more obvious marker for self-loathing than narcissism.

*

Shields: Two ideas are, I think, still—just barely—in circulation: Trump has or had "animal political genius" and "huge balls." Is either true?

*

Jones: I think of Trump as a really interesting philo-antisemite who, on some level, worships a certain Jewish style of verbal engagement, which he learned, first of all, from his lawyer and his father's lawyer, Roy Cohn, and from, of course, Howard Stern. It's impossible to overestimate the degree to which his verbal pyrotechnics are a kind of mashup of Roy Cohn aggression and Howard Stern performativity. And so, even though Trump pretends to be freestyle and improv, and he's always breaking from his written script, and he can't bear to read verbatim what has been written for him, he's incredibly rigorous about this one idea that got banged into his head by Roy Cohn and at a different register by Howard Stern—which is: always, always, always, always, always be the aggressor. Always be on the attack, never answer the question, never be on the defensive, always be attacking and always have a stalking horse. Never be for something. Always be against something. Never explain. Never apologize. Never ask for love.

Just think of the opening moment of Trump's election campaign, when he comes down that gold-plated elevator surrounded by paid actors who are there to applaud him; and then, as we all know, his very first gesture was to attack so-called Mexican rapists, etc. Again, always have an attack. Trump is extraordinarily rigorous about that. Meanwhile, the Democrats are still going on as if this were 1967 and we were living in some sort of civil society. Trump has shifted the Overton window; he's changed how conversation exists in a public sphere. The discourse might revert back after he's gone, or it might not. But that is Trump's rhetorical pattern. It never varies.

*

Jones: Obviously, his speaking style is fully on display at his rallies. His rallies are pure Goebbels. They are great theater. And the thing is, he does them in places that don't get a lot of theater. He goes into outlying areas across the country; in other words, he doesn't hold rallies in affluent suburbs or major cities. They're like WWE events, and they're entertaining. I've watched a lot of them, and I feel guilty that I'm entertained.

*

At a media avail: *The fact is—you people won't say this, but I'll say it: I was a much better candidate than her. You always say she was a bad candidate. You never say I was a good candidate. I was one of the greatest candidates ever. Nobody else would've beaten the Clinton machine, as crooked as it was. But I was a great candidate. One day you're going to say that.*

Jones: Trump pushes all the existential questions right into our fucking faces.

Shields: I recently did a podcast with Bret Ellis, and it occurred to me that Trump is Patrick Bateman, the antihero of *American Psycho*: someone who reflects back to us our worst self, our most "real self," all our guiltiest and darkest secrets.

*

Shields: The possibility often occurs to me that he's intentionally mirroring his base's permanent sense of *ressentiment*. If so, this is genius.

*

Bill Maher: "It's because everything is so unfair. His favorite word is 'unfair.' He's the luckiest guy in the world and he's got this chip on his shoulder. That's what I don't understand. His whole attitude is, *When will white men born to great wealth finally catch a break in America?*"

*

Jones: Heisenberg's Uncertainty Principle states that "the perceiver by his very presence alters what's perceived." Trump goes, *Fuck yeah, I'm gonna quadruple down on this.*

*

William Deresiewicz: "'Fact,' etymologically, means 'something done'—that is, an act or deed—a sense that still survives in phrases like 'accessory after the fact.' It was only in the sixteenth century—an age that saw the dawning of a new empirical spirit, one that would issue not only in modern science but also in modern historiography, journalism, and scholarship—that the word began to signify our current sense of 'real state of things.'"

*

Trump: *You see, I think I'm right, and when I think I'm right, nothing bothers me.*

*

Shields: E. L. Doctorow asks, "If justice cannot be made to operate under the worst possible conditions of social hysteria, what does it matter how it operates at other times?" At a symposium celebrating his work, an assistant professor asked him whether he saw any connection between the conflation of fact and fiction present in his historical novels and this statement to Ron Suskind made by an unnamed Bush 43 aide (widely believed to be Karl Rove): "We're an empire now, and when we act, we create our own reality. While you're studying that reality—judiciously, as you will—we'll act again, creating other new realities, which you can study, too; that's how things will sort out. We're history's actors, and you, all of you, will be left to just study what we do."

It's easy to mock Doctorow for being offended and refusing to answer, but what do I do with the correlation Adam Kirsch made, in the *Atlantic*, between the emptying out of genres that my book *Reality Hunger* advocates and embodies and the "free with the facts" approach that Michael Wolff took in *Fire and Fury*? Am I okay with that? Sort of. Sort of not. (Is this my "afterguilt"?)

Stephen Marche, in the *Los Angeles Review of Books*, says something different but related: "In a world turned upside down by reality hunger, *Reality Hunger* needs to be turned upside down, too. The post-fact world no longer demands, as the condition of creative fluidity, a rush away from the tyranny of facts, as Shields imagined. Rather the opposite..."

Shields: Q.v. the ubiquitous commercial for the *New York Times*: "The truth has power. The truth will not be threatened. The truth has a voice." Michael Medved said, "Sooner or later, there is such a thing as reality." To me, that's the key question—is there? I'm against "alternative facts," I suppose, but I'm for "alternative interpretations." Trump, et al. are, obviously, post-postmodernism incarnate; it's as if they've taken all post-1968 French deconstruction (and anemic American attempts to follow French deconstruction) and transformed it into a key element of political stagecraft. How conscious is the translation of all this theory into praxis?

*

Jeet Heer: "The visual has triumphed over the literary, fragmented sound bites have replaced linear thinking, nostalgia has replaced historical consciousness, simulacra are indistinguishable from reality, an aesthetic of pastiche and kitsch has replaced modernism's striving for purity, and a shared culture of vulgarity papers over intensifying class disparities."

*

Jones: Why, in the immediate aftermath of 9/11, did the Bush-Cheney administration not quite embrace full fascism? Adam McKay's film *Vice* focuses heavily on how much of Cheney's attempt to be a tough guy was to try to please the unpleasable Lynne Cheney. Dick just wants to be a man in Lynne's eyes, so he's gonna blow up the world. And apparently Trump has a small dick, and he wants people to worship him. You know, Hitler was impotent;

Mao was impotent; Saddam was impotent; Gandhi was impotent. Their impotence doesn't explain everything, but it matters.

*

David Wojahn: "Fascists, like poets, care deeply for the power of words; they love the slipperiness and instability of language, love the formal challenge of hammering falsehood into received wisdom, just as poets love the nuanced intricacies of turning 140 syllables of rhymed pentameter into a sonnet."

*

Shields: Trump's misspellings (e.g., "unpresidented," "State of the Uniom," "Special Council," "Teresa May," "Air Force Once," "Marine Core," "Melanie is feeling and doing really well") may have begun, decades ago, by accident, but now they're clearly purposeful—major base-build.

*

Maher: "Illiteracy isn't Trump's shame; it's his bond."

*

Jones: There's performative legerdemain there, for sure. I often wonder, does Trump just come up with this stuff on the spot? Does he plan it? Does somebody write it for him? That McCain line—"I prefer my heroes not to be captured"—is an amazing and very funny and very nasty line. And it carries resonance. It's an approach that goes back quite deep in Republican political thinking: you go after, say, Kerry by even denying that Kerry was a war hero, and then everything else falls away. The statue no longer exists.

Shields: It starts with the inauguration. "No, those photographs aren't true, our inauguration was in fact bigger than Obama's…" There is no reality. Now, when we look back on it, he couldn't have fired a more overt starting gun for his presidency. That photograph you saw? No, that's meaningless, that's fake news. That's the failing *New York Times*. And for the last several years, it's been simply an incremental extension.

*

Jones: In *Reality Hunger*, you say anything processed by memory is fiction, and so that book has a kind of postmodern tone. But you're not a complete relativist, are you? I mean, you think there *are* truths, don't you? Discoverable truths? Andrew Sullivan talks about how postmodernity taught us to interrogate the stories we tell, and he thinks that liberalism can incorporate postmodernity and critical theory but that critical theory can't incorporate liberalism. Sullivan says that classical liberalism has room for lots of different kinds of discourse. Generally, the people who were telling the postmodern story were left of center, in the interest of giving voice to people who were marginalized. It's fascinating that someone (Trump) who stands against everything that the postmodern view would sympathize with has turned postmodernity on its head. And I don't know how you put the toothpaste back in the tube at this point. Because this is not going away. Republicans who think, *oh, we made our Faustian bargain, and then we'll take the party back*: no. The Republicans have kind of wed themselves to the "no truth" reality.

Shields: The strategy is to bamboozle people with so much information and so many competing narratives—to say at 2 p.m. something that you contradict at 3 p.m.—that after a while people give up, and they have no idea where truth is. And to what degree is there an intellectual cadre behind Trump who has taught him to do this vs. to what degree does this all come pretty naturally to him? I think it's the latter. He's been a bullshit artist since he was born.

*

Jones: Trump says, *I'm not just offering you an excessive moment; I'm offering you an excessive world.* The media are wrong. Science is wrong. The liberals are wrong. What does Jesus say when he heals people or when he delivers someone marginalized and oppressed from their suffering? He says, I'm bringing you into the kingdom of heaven. This is an alternate reality. Well, Trump does that as the anti-Christ. A sort of Cyrus figure. He says, This is even better than just having beers with your buddies once a week and making some racist comments. I'm gonna give you a world where you can make the racist comments and wear the MAGA hat all week. We're gonna make America great again. We're gonna make *America* the excess.

Shields: He's very "Lacanian." All "lack," all "excess." Trump forces lack into people. But how does he accomplish that? What role does "lack" play in Trump's equation?

Jones: I think he knows that he's lacking and that we're all lacking. America's lacking. The most powerful nation in the world is somehow a sucker nation.

Shields: It's right there in "Make America Great *Again*," which suggests that America has fallen. That's lack. "Make it *Great* Again"—that's excess. Lack and excess show up right there in those four words.

Jones: "Again" even offers people a fantasy. When was the last time this country was great? It should just be "Make America Great."

Shields: Well, we're talking about Paradise Lost: America was once a nation of white people, of white men. I think that's the crucial move. That it was once okay, in the Eisenhower '50s, or the Jeffersonian 1790s, to conceive of a nation of white men. "Again" clearly plays on that.

Jones: In 2020, Trump had everyone convinced that there were mass balloting problems. In Philadelphia, for example, it's a fact that there were Republican and Democratic ballot observers, but they couldn't get closer than six feet because of Covid. And so he was pointing to Covid restrictions and saying, *Our people got shut out*. But, no, that's ridiculous. The Democrats didn't have more access than the Republicans did. *No one* could look over shoulders, as they could pre-Covid. But to be on the team, you have to believe it. You have to believe these superstitions. And the creeds get longer and longer. You have to believe this misinformation about climate change; you have to believe these QAnon conspiracies. It's fascinating what becomes more and more mainstream.

If they want to convince people to believe in superstition, Fundamentalist Christian preachers should be going to QAnon seminars (do these still exist?), because it's genius the way QAnon compelled people to believe its doctrines. Utter genius.

Shields: All the existentialists and proto-existentialists (from Melville to Nietzsche to Sartre) have basically said, *Civilization is the thinnest of veneers*; Trump just goes ahead and embodies the truth of this. It's kind of amazing.

Jones: But he does it like a four-year-old would do it. It's ultimately not fulfilling for him (or his followers). You and I probably couldn't live in that space, giving into that much animal impulse.

Shields: Right, it's *I have a trophy wife; I don't even pretend to care about my children; I'm terrified of death*. I do think he understands that we're animals—nothing more, nothing less.

*

Jones: What I'm fascinated by is the retreat of the left to Platonism. For the last forty years, you've had all these people on the cultural right publishing books on the dangers of postmodernism and the dangers of relativism (Allan Bloom's *The Closing of the American Mind*; Lynne Cheney's catastrophizing that perspectivalism is going to end Western civilization), and now you have Trump weaponizing this perspectivalism, which sends the left careening, in retreat, back to old-school objectivity. And that move seems to me so intellectually bankrupt. It's bad faith on both sides.

Shields: Yes, it's hilarious. Fox News and News Nation could not be more "everything is relative."

Jones: And now the left sounds like Allan Bloom.

Shields: Exactly. Right before the 2018 elections, Trump was hovering over the mid-terms—he was hovering over everything—and I was working on a project that revolved around interviewing teachers of nonfiction writing from around the country, about forty people who have been raised (as have I) on poststructuralism and deconstructionism. And they said they wanted to embrace perspectivalism, but they knew when they did so they sounded Trumpian. And that's where it gets interesting, because your options on the left are either to retreat into a Bloomian "there is a capital-T truth" position, which is epistemologically moribund, or a *Reality Hunger*-ish perspectivalism, which sounds like a roadmap for Trumpian malfeasance.

When people ask me if books like *Reality Hunger* paved the way for Trump, I don't have an easy answer. Is there a kind of intellectual giving up in *Reality Hunger* that goes, *Hey, there is no truth, may the best story win*? And if so, is that wrong? What's your take on all this?

Jones: I'm sympathetic to "the best story wins."

Shields: I am, too, apparently.

Jones: The modernists—Eliot, Joyce, Woolf, et al.—knew there were no foundations. They knew we were floating in the ether and that *stories* are all we have.

Shields: "Exciting." "Fun." Scary.

Jones: And wouldn't it be dishonest and in bad faith to go back on that intellectual history just because Trump told a compelling story to the country? That's what I find disingenuous—to disown what I think is the fruition of a lot of late-modern intellectual labor because you're frustrated that Trump won.

Shields: You can't discard Nietzsche due to Hitler. You can't even discard Heidegger. You'd have to discard Kierkegaard; you'd have to discard Hegel. Because Nietzsche is, in a way, the end of one intellectual tradition and the beginning of another.

*

James Parker: "Trump can't go off message because his message is, *Look at me—I'm off message*."

*

Sebastian Heid: "A proper relativist would have to say that all stories are equally valid, since all stories can always at best only capture one point of view and there is no objective truth behind the narratives, anyway. We might have only narratives, but the fact that we have several versions of the same story allows us to do some speculative triangulations of the motives and attitudes of the characters."

*

Slavoj Žižek: "The ongoing rise of populism is grounded for many ordinary people in the experience, 'Don't believe what the government or public media are telling you.' It's a general mistrust, and I think this is a quite justified mistrust. This is how our entire culture is changing. Today, more and more in our public debate, we have this multicultural, multi-truth approach. The idea is that it's oppressive even to mention that sometimes there is one truth. Every subject—especially if a 'victim'—has the right to say its own truth, and we have no right to disqualify it. This very culture of identity politics creates a kind of relativization in which you're no longer able to criticize anyone. Instead of proposing an alternate vision of how to change things, all the left is doing, or at least what they're doing in the most convincing way, is making fun, demonstrating the stupidity, of Trump. All the big problems that we see today—the explosion of new populism, ecological disaster, and so on: Trump is the reaction. Trump is, as they say, an effect and not a cause. Fighting just Trump is what doctors call 'symptomal healing.'"

*

Peter Pomerantsev: "The postmodern politician doesn't just bend the truth, as his predecessors did, but fundamentally subverts the idea that there is any knowable, objective truth at all. Putin and Trump's undermining the possibility of establishing reality is tactically clever; they thus remove the space in which one can make a rational case against them. Criticism becomes lost in a fog of unknowing. Maybe Putin and Trump's postmodernist disdain for objective facts is part of their appeal. Facts are, after all, unpleasant things; they tell you that you're going to die, that you might not be good-looking, rich, or clever. They remind you of your limitations. There is a rebellious joy in throwing off the weight of them."

*

Shields: I'm fascinated by the *New York Times* advertising slogan "The truth matters," as if somehow the *Times*, which gets almost everything wrong—they always get stuff right about ten years late—protects the official truth for us, and also as if "the truth matters" is somehow now the mantra of the left and center-left. Huh? "The truth"? We should now believe in one capital-T truth? I literally don't get it. How did the right become the postmodern party while the left became the party of pre-modernism?

Shields: Obama liked to say over and over that "perfect is the enemy of good," which meant, in practice, *I don't have to try so hard because change only happens incrementally, and we're all going to be dead, anyway*, whereas Trump says, *I'm perfect, and good is the enemy.*

Jones: Or maybe in that paradigm Trump is also the good—*I'm perfect, and I'm good.*

Shields: Brazenness has for a while (going back to at least Lee Atwater) been the cardinal Republican virtue; you demonstrate your seriousness by the depth and range of your brazenness.

Jones: Obfuscating his contradictions is the truth for Trump. He contradicts himself all the time, but no truth comes from it. Everything that comes out of his mouth is bullshit. In Harry Frankfurt's *On Bullshit*, he says the liar is morally superior to the bullshitter because at least the liar has to know the truth to make the lie, whereas the bullshitter doesn't need to know whether he's telling the truth. And Trump doesn't know what's true or not, which is why he's so effective. The bullshitter also, of course, bullshits himself.

*

Jones: After the incidents in Charlottesville, Trump held a ninety-minute press conference, and John Podhoretz said, "I don't know why Trump doesn't do this three times a week—not that it would be great for the country, but for his own ego and pleasure. He's never happier than when he's at a rally or sparring with the press."

Shields: When someone from the press tries to interrupt or talk over him or push back, he inevitably goes, "Excuse me, excuse me, excuse me." Basically, *I was talking; how dare you interrupt me,* when the person was just trying to ask a question. Rhetorically, it's very effective.

He's partially right when he says something like, "Thomas Jefferson owned slaves, George Washington owned slaves. Are we going to pull all those statues down as well?" I think that's an interesting question, and I don't have the answers, but at what point does the virtue-signaling revisitation of American history end? His cognitive ability has declined precipitously, but at one point he was awfully good at this sort of jousting with the media.

Jones: As a progressive person, I say this in a sympathetic voice, but the censoriousness of the cultural left is striking. Maher was disinvited from Berkeley for the supposed close-mindedness of something he said about female genital mutilation in Islam-majority countries. So, it seems like Trump gets his finger on the pulse; he feels the censoriousness and gives people permission to speak: *You can speak; we can speak; they're not the elite; we've got bigger houses, better apartments, we're better-looking here in Topeka* (or wherever). But, again, the left has made this. The left has opened a space for someone to come in and leverage their censoriousness against them.

Shields: He knows how to listen to his own nerve endings the way a good autobiographical writer does. He knows how to listen to his own vital, visceral, pseudo-Nietzschean feelings. He feels things very primitively. *I just feel that Obama wasn't born here, and I'm just gonna go with it…* or *Obama's a Muslim*, or *he snuck into Harvard Law*. Many of the promptings are wrong, but then some of the promptings are right (like *Where does the revisitation of American history end?*). Some of the promptings are crazy, but he just leans into them, and he knows the car crash is always more interesting than the smooth-running highway.

*

Shields: We're all listening to post-rock albums and post-truth podcasts, visiting post-figurative painting exhibitions, watching post-drama theater, reading post-plot lit, and yet we're supposed to be surprised that we no longer have conviction-led politics? We're being told "stories"? The feigned shock is beyond risible. The dissection enacts the very phenomenon it's pretending to dissect. My students clamor for an explanation for the disorientation they feel.

*

Parker: "Trump's speaking style is from the future, from a time to come when human consciousness has broken down into little floating atavistic splinters of subjectivity and superstition and jokes that aren't really jokes."

*

Shields: *Moby-Dick* is about how there is no longer any God; the whiteness of the whale is the abyss of a godless universe. In a way, you could link Trump to an impulse that started with Melville and Nietzsche, and then certainly Dostoevsky, coming up to the twentieth century, with Wittgenstein and Saussure, and quantum physics, poststructuralism, semiotics, postmodernism. When Giuliani said, "Truth isn't truth," he was mocked. But of course, that concept has been the intellectual default for easily the last hundred years. It's still not clear to me if people like, say, Steve Bannon have read a little academic theory and passed it up the food chain. In other words, how did Giuliani know to say, "Truth isn't truth"?

Jones: I think there's an undeniable link; from Nietzsche all the way through Derrida, you have one huge immersion in subjectivity and, in a way, meaninglessness.

*

Shields: Everyone knows how much Trump has learned from tabloid media, reality TV, WWE. What exactly has he learned, though?

*

Shields: Here is Trump's exchange with Bill O'Reilly after Trump said he "respected" Putin as a leader—

O'Reilly: But he's a killer.

Trump: There are a lot of killers. You think our country's so innocent? I think our country has plenty of killers, also.

This is a nearly exact, quite conscious, and purposeful echo of this moment in *The Godfather*:

Michael (Al Pacino) says to Kay (Diane Keaton), "My father's no different than any other powerful man—any man who's responsible for other people, like a senator or a president."

Kay: "You know how naïve you sound?"

Michael: "What?"

Kay: "Senators and presidents don't have men killed."

Michael: "Who's being naïve, Kay?"

Jones: Trump's explicit instruction to his White House staff was to structure each day as a long reality TV episode that he winds up winning.

*

Shields: Even before he became president, Trump promised drama. He pretended that if Hillary got elected, we would have a series of investigations (into her supposed crimes), but what Trump promised (and delivered) was entertainment. Obviously, it's the greatest reality TV show ever produced. That's a big lesson he learned from *The Apprentice*: that you have to incrementally ratchet up the drama every day. And, in a way, he has produced amazing ratings. CNN couldn't be happier, MSNBC, NPR, PBS, the *New York Times*—they're all just eating at the Trumpian trough.

Jones: A few years ago, he gave a speech to the UN in which he claimed that his administration had accomplished more in the previous two years than any other administration in the history of the republic, and all the diplomats laughed. Trump broke character and just started laughing, too, as if in acknowledgement of how fictional that claim was. To me, it was a rather pure tell that Trump does know that he's spinning pure fiction, that he knows he's lying every second of every day.

*

Shields: One thing he really understands that a lot of people on the left and center-left and in the media and in standard discourse don't understand is that politics have now become completely symbolic theater; the policies are quite secondary or even tertiary.

Neil Postman's *Amusing Ourselves to Death* is a good if rather simple-minded book about television; I do think that phrase captures what Trump knows to be true about our society—that we live in a dying culture; that we are hyperaware of our human mortality; that there are pockets of quasi-religiosity in the culture but, in many ways, we are living rather secularized lives; and that he's going to deliver amusement.

Jones: Apparently, he—but only he—can do whatever he wants.

Shields: During the Reagan Administration, *60 Minutes* ran a Reagan campaign ad and showed how the rhetoric of the images was at utter odds with the actual policies enacted. Reagan's press secretary called up CBS and thanked it for running their campaign ad for free. The critique doesn't matter; no one pays attention to the words.

Jones: Forty years later, Trump understands, far better than Reagan did, how visual we are. But the reason Trump's performances work is that if you watch someone like Jerry Nadler or Chuck Schumer on cable TV, they speak in constant euphemism; they speak in utterly vetted, corporatized language; they speak an odd kind of pseudo-liberal, quasi-humanist mumblecore, and so Trump feels, by comparison, like a prison break.

Shields: Asked, in one interview, "How do you handle this media storm?" he said, "I *am* the storm."

*

Shields: Several years ago, I was giving a reading from my book *Nobody Hates Trump More Than Trump*; someone came up to me afterward and said, "Trump is an assault on discourse itself." That seems to me key. Trump understands politics is revenge by any means necessary. For Trump's base, it's pure blood sport.

Jones: Americans have taken up perspectivalism, or poststructuralism, to make the argument that if you're gay you have a perspective; if you're a woman; if you're Black, etc. So, what is Trump's big move? Trump says, *This is great: everyone's got a perspective; mine's the best.*

Shields: In American academic circles, perspectivalism had a moral telos. It was an attempt at inclusion. Traditionalists who critiqued it were saying, *Look, you can go too far with this; if everything is permissible*.... But the people who were doing the work had a putative moral center.

Jones: Now, if you give someone like Trump this perspectivalist weapon, it's like giving a six-year-old a chainsaw.

Shields: There's no way he's read even a paragraph by, say, Žižek or Houellebecq. In 1986, he was just this playboy who would criticize the Central Park Five. So how did he learn this very specific strategy, which Giuliani, Kellyanne Conway, Bannon, Stephen Miller, and Putin all seem to follow, which is to always counter with, "That's just what *you* say"? How did they learn to do that? Did it just sort of seep into the water over a generation or two?

Jones: In *The Loudest Voice*, which is about Roger Ailes, you get an idea of what happened. During Walter Cronkite's time, Americans would supposedly stand around the water cooler, and we might have different opinions, but there was a general consensus that ABC, CBS, NBC, the *Wall Street Journal*, the *New York Times*, PBS—these are the facts, and we have different opinions, but we all have the same facts, more or less. These are news outlets that we consider actual sources.

There's a great scene in *The Loudest Voice* when the suits are pitching the idea for Fox News; Rupert Murdoch is in the room, and someone says, "We're going to do a show like *A Current Affair*, but it's gonna be edgier." Roger Ailes says, "That seems to me incredibly stupid." The others say, "What do you mean?" Ailes says, "Half of America doesn't have a voice. Let's give them a news voice that's conversative and has a pro-American message." The birth of Fox News.

I think most mainstream media people try to be fair. Does that mean they're unbiased? No. Everybody's biased. I have my own biases, but I can be fair. I'll try to give an honest analysis while acknowledging my biases. But I think Fox depends on the premise that there is no such thing as fairness—except Fox itself. "Fair and Balanced."

Shields: Which was always meant to be ironic. It was meant to be mocking.

Jones: They put Juan Williams on *The Five* and kicked the shit out of him. *See, we had a liberal; it was balanced.* I think Fox News is a big part of how they all learned the strategy you're talking about.

Shields: Quoting my friend Nina Goss here: "But 2024 is not an unprecedented insane asylum; I am not the Smart and Good watching the Moronic and Evil take over; I'm not even the passive, sleeping Good letting the Evil take over. This is the continual agon of Western skepticism. Trump, Bannon, and Conway are events in the history of truth/meaning and not underworld, nonhuman spawn who, oh my god, are ruling my world."

Immanuel Kant: "Out of the crooked timber of humanity, no straight thing was ever made."

*

Trump associate: "He is the most present human being I have ever met. He lives entirely in the moment. He doesn't define himself through relationships or through some spiritual interests or concerns. He defines himself and redefines himself from day to day by what happens in his life."

*

Shields: Trump floats outlandish ideas, e.g., a military parade for himself, and then if/when they get shot down/shut down, he always says he was just joking. Nobody in the history of American politics has been able to do this. How does he do it? It's because it's a given, on all sides of the discourse, that the entire operation is a sham. Everyone knows it and yet no one says this, exactly, because the "right" loves the anti-establishmentarian audacity of the WWE spectacle—the kayfabeness of it—and the "left" fulminates, apoplectically and completely counterproductively (utterly symbiotically), and the entire cycle continues, minute by minute, the meter never not clicking over.

*

Shields: *Kayfabe*—is that a term you know? I guess carnies use the term at carnivals. It's basically pig Latin for "fabulous, okay?" What *kayfabe* refers to is that carnies think that people who go to carnivals know that the games are totally rigged, and that they know that if they throw a little ring toward a disc, it's not going to land, but it's fun to be part of this fiction together. It's fun to enter this fictional space of the carnival. It doesn't matter if the basketball you shoot goes in the basket. It almost certainly is not going to go into the basket at the carnival, but there's kind of a mutual agreement to enter a fictional space, or the realm of what is now called (and I think it's a really useful term) "fan fiction." To what degree is Trump aware of this? I think he's fully aware of how much he's fulfilling all these desires that we've talked about. I would call him "hyper-performative."

*

Tim Parks: "Liberals don't get how much Trump is their child. Trapping us up for so long in their correctness, their can't-offend, their sense of guilt, they created their monstrous opposite. The #metoo movement is an exacerbation of the same spiral. All men suddenly feel they have to apologize for being men, all whites for being whites, etc. And suddenly people love an appalling guy who won't apologize and champions whites."

*

Louis Theroux: "For all Trump's awfulness, I can't help but admire his shamelessness, in an odd way. Or maybe not admire but be fascinated by it and maybe envy it. In a shame culture, he seems to have figured out that if you refuse to be shamed, it gives you enormous power."

*

Shields: Sometimes the values that reign in academic/literary culture seem completely divorced from the values that reign in the Trumpian universe, but in actuality they're utterly interdependent and reinforcing.

Shields: Anything—anything—is better than NPR's onesy-twosy earnestness. I literally can't listen to it anymore. Anything—anything—is more appealing than Ari Shapiro's instantaneous, ersatz empathy on NPR. This is where Trump comes in—

*

Andrew Altschul: "Trump has gleefully ripped away the pitiful veneer of 'genteel society'—how full of shit so many people on the left are, not because they're wrong per se but because they're so committed to an Oprah-ized, airbrushed, focus-grouped, ultimately empty language in which they can't convince anyone of anything anymore. For me, the absolute avatar of this is John Kerry, who hasn't spoken a word from his heart/gut since those 1971 Congressional hearings. 'Liberals' reduce even the most urgent political issue (e.g., health care, gun control, etc.) to soggy politesse and etiquette and meaningless word packages. This is why they always lose; they're playing badminton, and the Republicans are playing ice hockey. It's enough to make us wish someone would come along and just say whatever the fuck he thinks, even if we disagree with him.

"Ever since 1994 (Gingrich), Republicans have been willing to commit any kind of hypocrisy, break any tradition, smear anyone, lie about anything, bend any rule, exploit any loophole, and generally shrug at any protocol that's an impediment to winning. The Democrats have always been far more concerned about their supposed integrity, which all too often results in not taking clear shots when they have them, not responding in kind to the most egregious kneecapping, and generally getting hung up on procedural/traditional points.

"Perfect example: During the Bush 43 administration, Republicans were beating them up for filibustering Bush's judicial appointees and threatened 'the nuclear option' unless the Dems loosened their chokehold. Instead of daring them to do it, the Dems caved, in exchange for the promise—which was utterly meaningless—that the Republicans would never use the nuclear option themselves and would preserve the Dems' ability to filibuster Supreme Court appointees. Fast-forward ten years, when the Dems really needed to be able to stop the appointment of Gorsuch, which had become possible only because of the GOP's nihilistic refusal to fulfill their responsibilities on Obama's Garland nomination. Of course, the GOP used the nuclear option to make sure its nominee would be confirmed. Anyone who thought the GOP would hold its fire in the name of Senate tradition or fair play is an idiot. The fact that the Democrats insist on playing this game is why they've been losing political power since LBJ."

It's Lucy and Charlie Brown and the football. It's also sadism and masochism.

*

Shields: All this entertainment, all of this "transgression," began to feel beside-the-point in the face of a worldwide pandemic. You could hardly have contrived a more perfect counterpoint to Trumpian fabrication; it's straight out of *Oedipus at Colonus*: a plague was unleashed upon the land.

Jones: Liberal society is complicated because there are always boundaries and limitations on our speech. Liberals are never going to sanction all speech. And so there's often a kind of pendulum swing. Or it's like tuning an old-school radio; it's easier to find the static than it is to find the pure station. And I think that's part of the struggle, too. Because again, there are voices of postmodernity and critical theory that are saying, rightly, I think, *Look, there are some forms of speech that are profoundly harmful, in ways we didn't historically think about because certain people were marginalized.* But then how do you put that in conversation with a liberal spirit that says, *Look, it's often the offensive idea that probably needs a hearing.* And I think there are real tensions there. We're at the same time a more permissive culture and a less forgiving culture. We're not more gracious. The permissiveness has come with a censorious side—the whole cancel culture dimension. So I think that's the struggle. And I think people feel the challenge of negotiating that space. And Trump just says, *Blow it up.* He shamelessly and theatrically opens the release valve that people are looking for because *I don't know how to negotiate this,* and *I'm getting judged for saying this,* and *I didn't mean anything bad.*

*

Simon Gray: "But finally no man can speak for the tumult of his time unless he speaks from the tumult of himself"—what Trump either does or pretends to do, or does without knowing it, or all three (which gives it its immense frisson).

*

Shields: While in most people the dominant win/lose American paradigm is tempered by the feeling that to really win, one needs also to be good, Trump is simply uninterested in that and believes winning is winning regardless of being good—which comes as a great relief to many people who feel held back by trifling moral concerns.

Shields: What Trump does is he shows you how bored he is; he also knows how to *pretend* to act excited; he also shows you the space between the boredom and the excitement; it's a never-ending feedback loop, and the viewer is clued in every second—which feels flattering, fun.

*

Oscar Wilde: "Man is least himself when he talks in his own person. Give a man a mask, and he will show you his true face."

*

Parker: "For the early punk bands, not being able to play their instruments was a mark of virtue—a blow against the elites, the puffy-haired technocrats with their pointless 12-minute guitar solos."

*

Shields: I've said to my friend Keith Kopka that I like how punk pretends to be nihilistic but seems to me to hold out real hope, perhaps, in the deepest, darkest, most urgent and serious and earnest ways and places.

Kopka: "Trump has only the destructive side of punk down: the immature, selfish, myopic version. I'm trying to think what band Trump would be if he were a punk band; I see him fitting in nicely with the self-destructive narcissism of GG Allin and The Murder Junkies. In the '90s, record labels were looking to cash in on the success of bands like Green Day and Blink 182 that seem similar to this kind of manufactured rebellion. In the mall, you could buy denim jackets with anarchy patches already sewn onto them. At the time, this bothered me, and it still bothers me.

"However, Trump is actually much closer to the Sex Pistols: a band idolized and revered for helping to create the genre. They were messy. They didn't play by the rules. They upset political norms. They're remembered as an authentic entity. And they were 100% fabricated and manicured into existence by Malcolm McLaren, who really just wanted to sell fetish clothing. They were completely manufactured and wildly successful, which allowed them to remain or become willfully unaware of their own fakeness. At least initially, the Pistols didn't really think about the role that McLaren played in packaging the band. They bought their own shtick and just started living it until the shtick was indivisible from their day-to-day lives. At the last Pistols show, Johnny Rotten (either finally getting it or knowing it all along) asked the audience, 'Ever get the feeling you've been cheated?'"

*

C. J. Polychroniou evokes "a line in which residents are standing, expecting to move forward steadily as they work hard and keep to all the conventional values, but their position in the line has stalled. Ahead of them, they see people leaping forward, but that doesn't cause distress, because it's (allegedly) 'the American way' for merit to be rewarded. What does cause real distress is what's happening behind them. They believe that 'undeserving people' who 'don't follow the rules' are being moved ahead of them by federal government programs they see as designed to benefit African-Americans, immigrants, and others they often regard with contempt."

*

John Gartner: "The demagogues—whether it's someone like Trump or Hitler or Milošević—manipulate people so that instead of being a German, you're an Aryan; instead of being a Rwandan, you're a Tutsi or Hutu; instead of being a Yugoslav, you're a Serb or Croat. Now it's our gene pool against their gene pool. Trump and his people just made it very explicit. Trump's basic theme is, 'I am the alpha male of the white people. If you want to live, follow me,' and they did."

*

Jones: The substitution metaphor in the Bible doesn't begin at the cross; it begins at the earliest part of the Jesus story. "Gospel of Mark": Jesus goes into desolate places to pray; he encounters and heals lepers. *He'll be swamped, so don't tell anyone.* One of the lepers goes and tells people. Jesus is swamped. Then, according to Mark, Jesus had to stay in desolate places. Christ absorbed their pain. He died for the world's pains. *You absorbed my pain, Jesus; you died for our sins.*

Trump is basically saying to the people, *No, die for my sins*. In Trump's case it isn't one long march toward compassion; it's one long march toward narcissism. And what's powerful about it is that it reminds us of ourselves at our worst. In a way, all of us at our lowest common denominator are Trumpian narcissists.

*

Wilhelm Reich: "The average man's mind is structured for fascism."

*

Jason Stanley says, "Trump is an authoritarian who uses speech to define a simple reality that legitimates his value system, leading voters to adopt it. Its strength is that it conveys his power to define reality. Its weakness is that it obviously contradicts it. Denouncing Trump as a liar—or describing him as merely entertaining—misses the point of authoritarian propaganda altogether. Authoritarian propagandists are attempting to convey power by defining reality. The reality they offer is very simple. It's offered with the goal of switching voters' value systems to the authoritarian value system of the leader."

*

Mussolini, describing his countrymen: "A gesticulating, chatterbox, superficial, carnivalesque people."

*

According to Adam Curtis, "Vladislav Surkov is one of President Putin's advisors and has helped him maintain his power for fifteen years, but he has done it in a very new way. He came originally from the avant-garde art world, and those who have studied his career say that what Surkov has done is import ideas from conceptual art into the very heart of politics. His aim is to undermine people's perception of the world so they never know what's really happening. Surkov turned Russian politics into a bewildering, constantly changing piece of theater. He sponsored all kinds of groups, from Neo-Nazi skinheads to liberal human rights groups. He even backed parties that were opposed to Putin, but Surkov then let it be known that this was what he was doing, which meant no one was sure what was real or fake. As one journalist put it, it's a strategy to hold onto power by keeping all opposition constantly confused, a ceaseless shape-shifting that's unstoppable because it's indefinable. Which is exactly what Surkov is alleged to have done in Ukraine [in 2014]. In typical fashion, as the war began, Surkov published a short story about something he called Non-Linear War, in which you never know what the enemy is really up to, even who they are. The underlying aim, Surkov says, is not to win the war but to use the conflict to create a constant state of destabilized perception in order to manage and control."

*

Shields: Netflix's term for the algorithm it uses to predict what movie you want to watch is "pragmatic chaos."

*

Shields: Don Jr. said, "Russians make up a pretty disproportionate cross section of a lot of our assets." Therefore, Putin has nearly unlimited leverage over Trump. Might it also possibly be true that Trump loves being bullied by Putin in the way that Fred Trump bullied him? At the very least, it feels very, very familiar to Trump.

*

Shields: The Fox News online feed runs a constant drip of clips about Black people misbehaving: a high school teacher seducing her student, a nurse laughing at a World War II vet's request for CPR. Black people are extremely ungrateful for everything white people have done for them. Trump's election was a not-so-soft assassination of Obama. At the end of an article about Charlottesville, a reader commented, "It's okay to be white." An African-American reporter at the *NYT* once said to me, "We're all white supremacists—that's what we've been taught."

*

Shields: At a ceremony honoring Native-American World War II "code-talkers," Trump went out of his way to call Elizabeth Warren "Pocahantas." He always needs to empty out the moment, flatten it, piss on it (paying Moscow prostitutes to piss on a bed on which Obama slept; visiting a Vegas club called The Act, at which simulated golden showers were the key lure), turn glory or grace to shit, shit on it (instructing Stormy to spank him with an issue of *Forbes* on which he was the cover boy). Whence the origin of the drive? It matters whether it's political calculation (base-building), psychic need (destructiveness as suicide watch), or some combination, and if in combination, in what proportion. The answers aren't clear. I suppose most people don't care what the origins of this are for him, but I do. (This is still a detective story.)

*

Shields: Is it possible that Trump is a fake racist? If so, would this be better or worse than being a real racist?

*

Re the Central Park Five: *Of course I hate these people, and let's all hate these people because maybe hate is what we need if we're gonna get something done. I want to hate these muggers and murderers. They should be forced to suffer and, when they kill, they should be executed for their crimes.*

*

Trump, to US soldiers: *I'm financially brave.*

*

Shields: *ProPublica* released a tape of a six-year-old girl crying for her mother and father in a border detention center in Texas. Of course Trump wanted to separate children from their parents, destroying the kind of love he never got and can't experience.

*

Shields: *I have a great relationship with the Blacks.* It's impossible to overestimate the work done here by Trump's use of the word *the*; again, is he conscious of this, or is it his natural register, or is it his natural register and then is he aware of the value of not veering from that register?

*

Oh, look at my African-American over there.

*

We're worse than lions. At least they do it for food. We do it for the thrill of the hunt.

*

Jane Lynch, discussing Sue Sylvester, whom she played on *Glee*: "No one is that cock-sure unless she's hiding something."

*

Shields: Can one say, coherently, that one is a truly tolerant person if one refuses to tolerate intolerance? A tricky problem in logic, but there may be much riding on our ability to resolve it.

*

Adrian Wooldridge, political editor of the *Economist*: "A Manhattan-based playboy who has had life handed to him on a silver platter might look like a strange vehicle for the pain of the heartland, but Trump is a winner with the soul of a loser. He is consumed by imagined slights to his fragile ego, hypersensitive to the pretensions of smarty-pants liberals, a man who spends many hours a day watching cable news and seething with anger."

*

Tony Schwartz, "co-author" of *The Art of the Deal*: "From the very first time I interviewed him in his office in Trump Tower in 1985, the image I had of Trump was that of a black hole. Whatever goes in quickly disappears without a trace. Nothing sustains. It's forever uncertain when someone or something will throw Trump off his precarious perch—when his sense of equilibrium will be threatened and he'll feel an overwhelming compulsion to restore it. Beneath his bluff exterior, I've always sensed a hurt, incredibly vulnerable little boy who just wanted to be loved. What Trump craves most deeply is the adulation he has found so fleeting."

*

I love losers because they make me feel so good about myself.

*

Shields: We invent idols that contain the contradictions within ourselves. Ichiro, Madonna, Elvis, and Jesus, for example, are all somehow—simultaneously, impossibly—avatars of both absolute conformity and absolute rebellion.

*

Shields: Trump wards off his own suffering, which I think hugely connects him to his base, which is also suffering mightily. He helps them fight off their inner sadness. *Don't deal with your own pain, the failure of your job, your marriage, your psyche, your heart, your soul, but* (like a very lazy psychoanalytic patient) *always place the blame elsewhere*. Whereas Biden, of course, quadruples down on *I'm a suffering man*.

Jones: And don't you think it's no accident that Trump has all these rallies in opioid country?

Shields: That's a really good point.

Jones: He's an alternative opioid.

Shields: Right. The key is that we get an oceanic feeling, that surge—of what?—at a Trump rally . . .

Jones: The surge is white America. It's owning the libs. This is what Hitler was doing in Germany. It's a church language, but it's got to be less transcendent and more imminent. The real divinity is the *Volk*; it's the people. It's about being German. Fuck the French, who screwed us over at Versailles. France signed the Treaty of Versailles in a streetcar, and Hitler made France sign the surrender treaty *in* that streetcar. When they left the streetcar, Hitler blew it up. I mean, that's Trump. "The cruelty is the point."

Shields: I guess what's amazing about Trump is his emptiness—and then how he fills the emptiness with violation and violence. That's really interesting to me. The emptiness is clear; the violation is often sort of magisterial; and the violence is both verbal and pseudo-physical. That unholy trinity of emptiness, transgression, and revenge—those are three key moves in the Trump playbook.

I think it's a big problem that we can't talk about these dynamics, because remember when Obama gave that talk to some donors in the Bay Area in 2011, and he was asked, Why are people in rural Pennsylvania pro-God and pro-Guns and anti-Gay? (It's now God and Guns and Trump.) He was basically arguing that those things are metonyms for people's feelings of cultural irrelevance, but he had to walk it back because it was getting a little too close to the truth.

There are precedents: Jesse Ventura being the governor of Minnesota, Reagan being the governor of California and then the president of the United States, Schwarzenegger being the governor of California. These people had no prior political experience. *He was good at fake-wrestling and he has a deep voice and an authoritarian manner; let's elect him.* Partly as a goof, I think. *It'll be hilarious.*

Obama is very cold. He doesn't ever let you in. Trump is suffering *unmistakably*. Who else would talk for ten minutes about why he walked in a gingerly way down a ramp at West Point, or about the size of his hands, or feel the need to let the American people know that *I'm fine down there*. What other presidential candidate in the history of the world has said, *I have no problems down there*? Who could not hear how insecure that sounds?

Jones: But this is the sin of the garden. The story of the garden isn't about morality; it's about finitude. So what the serpent, the Satanic figure, does is he slithers in and asks, *Did God really say that? Did God really say that you're finite? Did God really say, if you eat from this…? Listen, you don't have these limits; you don't have these boundaries*. And isn't that what Trump does? *They say we can't get manufacturing back…* When he makes these claims, he denies American finitude; he denies that reality on the ground. We're not going to make the kind of products China makes; we can't afford it. It's impossible. The whole "Make America Great Again" concept is a denial of finitude. It's going back to the primal wound;

it's going back to the Garden of Eden, saying, *C'mon, c'mon, there are no limits here*. And so he's running around in opioid country, in Nebraska and Tennessee, and telling people that we're really going to get manufacturing back. I mean, do people really think we're going to become a manufacturing country again? He's making these claims that are so obviously, again, bullshit.

Shields: My favorite line from Madeline Miller's *The Song of Achilles*: "Name one hero who was happy." From Aquinas through Luther, up through Melville, Dostoevsky, Nietzsche, and onward: they were all sad as fuck and as a result they all, you might say, built a wall, the wall.

Jones: I think by the time we get to these nineteenth-century figures, the question is, Can we have the truth without God? You can have Christian truth, but by this point in history it's not going to be quite capital-T. It's going to be more existential. Or maybe you'll be an atheist. Or maybe you'll be a pluralist. Trump comes along and says, *Well, I'll give you God without the truth. I'll give you the godlike feeling of being at a religious rally. You don't have to read any Aristotle or worry about climate change or deficit spending or economic surplus. I'm God. I'm divinity.*

Shields: *I could kill someone on Fifth Avenue and not lose a single vote.*

Jones: The idea is that we don't *need* the truth anymore. "Blue states live red." If you live in a blue state, you might sign off on transgender story hour, but basically you live a pretty conservative lifestyle. The blue states have lower abortion rates, lower drug abuse rates, etc. If you're in a red state, you might be religious and right-wing, but there are higher teen-pregnancy rates in your state, and there's the opioid crisis. Trump becomes the balm in Gilead for all that. He comes in and tells you that all your struggles, your personal and family issues (which are compounded because we have all these systemic social issues), and all your anxiety about the economy—don't worry about it; it's *their* fault. We're making America great again, and we're going to get all these jobs back. You sort of give yourself permission to believe the lie. Again, the people who go to the rallies aren't idiots; they know the wall's not getting built. They're indulging a guilty pleasure. They're allowing themselves to be deceived because in the deception they get this psychic relief. *With all this pain, I can point to the people who are harming me: immigrants, liberals, coastal elites, etc.*

The thing that blows me away is that Hillary Clinton won only one-sixth of the counties in the entire country, but sixty-eight percent of the GDP was in those counties. The real question is, How are we *not* in a civil war yet?

Shields: Trump's narcissism, and vanity, and self-loathing, and self-indulgence are, in a way, the most interesting things about him because you have to ask to what degree Trump is consciously sculpting a persona that's going to resonate with a kind of emptied out lower-middle class. Or, for Trump, to what degree is there a sort of happy synergy between himself and a forgotten, white underclass? When he says *Nobody likes me*, I think that a lot of people in America who have been left behind feel very much the same way. Trump's brokenness isn't a problem; his brokenness, his woundedness, his narcissism, his vanity, his self-loathing are what connect him to his base, in that, they too are broken. They don't know why; they just like Trump. And it's utterly instructive to watch this open wound get turned, over and over and over again, into venom, anger, violence, and revenge (upon women, Black people, etc.).

Jones: Now, I think the tribal politics does our identity work for us. If you've got these open psychic wounds, politics is the blood sport that is your therapy. In other words, instead of grappling with your fear and anxiety, you go to the Trump rally or watch it on TV. And I have friends who are upper-middle class professionals; they're people who grew up in the posh suburbs of metro Philadelphia and New York, and they're not extremists, yet if they have a few drinks, and we're watching cable news, they sound like borderline white nationalists.

Shields: There are a lot of rules about what we can and can't say, and the kind of verbal violence that Trump delivers, the only reason that would resonate for you is if you had hugely underlying rage at, first of all, these monolithic institutions that tell you what to think (the *Times*, say,) and if you felt hugely straitjacketed by what the culture will and won't allow you to say. I think it's impossible to understand what Trump does without focusing on this phenomenon. The key thing isn't to say, *Oh, it's because Trump is entertaining; it's just more fun to listen to him than Hillary Clinton or Chuck Schumer or Joe Biden*; that's a given. (As Lorrie Moore has pointed out, there's an odd musicality to Trump's phrasings; he has a surprisingly high voice, which he plays like a musical instrument, and it does a complicated dance through different registers.) The key point for me is that not only is he, say, the anti-Obama or the anti-Hillary or the anti-Biden, and not only are we an amusing-ourselves-to-death society, but specifically that Trump empties out the official view of American history (whether it's mocking how we talk about John McCain as a war hero, or the standard approach to dealing with reporters, or the sanctioned way of talking about who the alleged killers are in a murder case); that's the core of Trump. He delivers something unbelievably sad, unbelievably wounded, but then he marries that incredibly effectively to free-floating anger.

*

Shields: At least once a week I think of that phrase of the historian Richard Slotkin's—"regeneration through violence": the perhaps peculiarly American mythology of purification through mayhem/blood/murder.

*

Shields: Some sort of bogus Emergency Expert showed up on NPR to claim that when we're watching disaster coverage we're doing so out of compassion/concern for our fellow citizens. This is utterly wrong. We watch to feel safe, wrapped in a cocoon of voyeurism and vicariousness and Schadenfreude. We like to see bad things happen to other people. This is terrible, but it's true. The clown Avner the Eccentric can easily walk straight between two trees on a slack rope, but for his act he wavers back and forth, mocks alarm, all but falls, and just makes it across. People dearly want him to fall. We will do anything to disrupt our lives. We worship chaos. It's impossible not to rubberneck.

*

Shields: It's pleasurable to participate in bloodshed but remain unconscious of our role in it.

*

Shields: My grandniece, a third-grader in Brooklyn Heights, explaining the insidious appeal of the class bully: "He's awful—everyone hates him—but he makes things more interesting."

Shields: When I asked a Jeb Bush policy advisor to tell me stories about what it was like to be part of a presidential campaign, she told me half a dozen anecdotes, each of which is a sort of earnest ode to the integrity, thoughtfulness, and idealism of the candidate. I literally can't comprehend how someone can think about other people this way. It's the same thing that made *The West Wing* impossible for me to watch. I think we are a fallen, doomed species. (Detective story.)

*

Jones: Trump is telling people in Middle America, *Absorb my sins, absorb my narcissism, absorb my tax policies,* which marginalize you and don't help you economically. *Absorb all this, and I will give you an emotional payoff.*

Shields: Which is what? We're back to lack and excess, for sure.

Jones: *We're gonna own the libs.*

Shields: That's all?

Jones: *We're gonna fucking own these people. You know, you might be sitting in a sub-standard home, but at least you've got your cable TV, and when you put my rally on, we're gonna stick it to those people in Manhattan and San Francisco and Seattle and Philadelphia. We're gonna screw them. We are gonna get them. I'm gonna make you feel less embarrassed about your religion, about being pro-life.* It's a huge emotional payoff.

Shields: Ever since the Kennedy assassination, we've been riveted to television in the hope we'll experience something equally traumatic, and I think Trump gets that very profoundly. I mean, who's going to watch a Biden press conference? Absolutely no one (until now, to watch him freeze). Whereas Trump, who knows what he might do? He might literally kill Jake Tapper. God is dead; let's party! It's *Ferris Bueller's Day Off, Dazed and Confused, The Big Lebowski*.

Jones: It's exhilarating.

Shields: Žižek's honest about that, as are, say, Houellebecq and Herzog and McGowan, and maybe I'm weirdly there, too.

*

People like a hero, a Golden Boy, but many like a fallen hero even better.

*

Shields: Everyone's ambition is underwritten by a tragic flaw. We're deeply divided animals who are drawn to the creation of our own demise. Freud says, "What lives wants to die again. The life-drive is in them, but the death-drive as well." (Notice that he says "them.") Milan Kundera writes, "Anyone whose goal is 'something higher' must expect someday to suffer vertigo. What is vertigo—fear of falling? No, vertigo is something other than fear of falling. It's the voice of the emptiness below us that tempts and lures us; it's the desire to fall, against which, terrified, we defend ourselves." And the more righteous our self-presentation, the more deeply we yearn to transgress, to fall, to fail—because being bad is more interesting, exciting, and erotic than being good. We all contrive different, wonderfully idiosyncratic, and revealing ways to remain blind to our own blindnesses.

Richard Nixon had to undo himself, because—as hard as he worked to get there—he didn't believe he belonged there. Biden now (in freefall), for sure. Bill Clinton's fatal charm was/is his charming fatality: his magnetism is his doom; they're the same trait. In short, what animates us inevitably ails us.

*

Bosley Crowther's *NYT* review in 1956 of Sir Laurence Olivier's *Richard III*: "Richard, the dark, misshapen monster of the English House of York in those medieval years when it was waging the War of the Roses with the stubborn Lancasters, is the towering focal figure in this complex drama of plots and murders at court. Sir Laurence's Richard is a weird, poisonous portrait of a super-rogue whose dark designs are candidly acknowledged with lick-lip relish and sardonic wit. He has an electric vitality and a fascinatingly grotesque grace. A grating voice, too, is a feature of his physical oddity.

"From a glib and egotistical conniver at the outset of the play, when he confides his clever purpose to the audience and hypocritically woos Lady Anne, he becomes a cold and desperate tyrant after he has ordered Clarence and Hastings dispatched and faces up to the horror of slaying the little princes in the Tower. And then, toward the end, he is lost of all feeling save terror and a horrible dread of his fate. Sir Laurence, as director as well as actor, has clearly and artfully contrived to emphasize Richard's isolation and his almost pathetic loneliness.

"No wonder one feels some sorrow for him—for this dark gangster of another age—when he dies on the ground, thrashing in torment, with spears sticking in him like a pig."

*

Shields: Trump knows there's nothing in this world that will save us. He made this incredible comment to Mark Singer thirty years ago for a *New Yorker* profile: *They can write anything they want about me. All that matters is a great piece of ass.* He's dancing in the abyss. That could hardly be more Nietzschean.

*

Shields: Trump is always playing Trump—fighting to win, but win what or why? He has no clue and knows he has no clue. And we know he has no clue. And he knows we know he has no clue. His lostness, his irreducible sadness, is what I find (or maybe used to find) so compelling, almost moving, about him.

*

Shields: Trying (failing) to adapt my book *Black Planet: Facing Race During an NBA Season* into a documentary film, the director said to me, "I think there's something a little bit scary about you. I like you a lot, but when I come close to you, I feel this desire on your part to just go after everything, including the things that both you and I love, and there are certain things that I don't want to destroy." (Good luck with that, pal.)

*

Shields: He hates himself, which is why he always projects onto his opponents all of his own sins. How crazy is the Trumpian projection? Part of the gaslighting is that you can't tell.

*

Robin Quivers [Howard Stern sidekick]: How do you feel about being a grandfather?

Trump: Not good.

Quivers: You don't let them call you "Grandpa"?

Trump: No, I don't. And I don't consider myself a grandfather. I don't even want to hear the term. There's nothing good about the clock.

*

Franz Kafka: "Miserliness is, after all, one of the most reliable signs of profound unhappiness. Nothing alive can be calculated."

*

Quivers: Are you a happy man, Donald?

Trump: Uh, yes, I think so. I mean, I like to say I'm a content man. I don't know if I'm capable of happiness, okay?

*

Jones: In general, he's comfortable with hatred. I would argue that the only thing that can save us from Trump's destructive qualities is his even more powerful impulse to self-destruct.

I think what's still underappreciated about Trump is the degree to which he thrives on chaos, which most people don't. He likes his employees to be squabbling; he intentionally puts them at war with each other. This is very echoic of the strife in Trump's family. He tries to replicate the relationship between his father and his father's children, in which they were endlessly squabbling for a little bit of Daddy's love, which took the form of money.

I had a paranoid thought several years ago, which has proven true, which is that I felt that Trump was intentionally allowing—hoping—that citizens in blue states would die during the pandemic, because he understood that especially at first a lot of people who were dying from Covid were Democrats in "sanctuary cities." Is it indifference or malevolence? I think on some fundamental level he simply doesn't care.

Shields: Adam Curtis, *The Century of the Self*.

Jones: He was like, *Fuck it; some people will die, but we'll get the economy going, it'll be fantastic*. He explained his behavior by saying he didn't want to panic people, but it's all always, obviously, about him.

Shields: His father taught him that one thing mattered: financial success. All there is is transactional capitalism. And rather than fight his father, who embodied all this, he internalized it and sends it out in quadruplicate to the rest of the world. Again, this is probably not conscious on his part, but he connects people to their own primitive urges through his rhetorical flourishes, rather like Steve Bannon calling for the beheading of Anthony Fauci at the height of Covid. The approach could hardly be more ancient and primitive.

Jones: Trump looks in the mirror and says, *I get more ratings, I get more everything*, I'll *tell you what's true*.

Shields: He has no belief in anything except transaction, which in a way is very Foucauldian. Everyone says, isn't that horrible, Trump is a transactionalist, *what can you do for me, what can I do for you* (hence his obeisance to Putin, because Putin knows that Deutsche Bank has a billion dollars over Trump's head, which got laundered through Russian and Eastern European offshore banking entities, etc., etc.). Foucault, though, is a total transactionalist, philosophically, whereas Trump takes the idea that we're all slave and master and says, *Yeah, I'm gonna fuck you over right now*. I would point out, though, at the end of Foucault's life, after he had contracted HIV/AIDS, he apparently didn't care if he fucked people to their death. That is so unbelievably Trump to me.

Jones: Around 2016, McGowan and Ryan Engley presented some work on the politics of power, and their critique of the left at the time was that the left was stuck in Foucault, where everything is a power dynamic, while Trump has actually evolved in some ways to Lacan—desire, the death wish, guilty pleasures. The idea is, you can't feel desire for Hillary Clinton or Joe Biden. It's eating your peas. It's cutting your cholesterol. McGowan's point is that when Trump says, *We're building the wall*, they know that no one's building a goddamn wall. But that's the desire. *Yeah, we don't care, and we know it's not true.* He's giving people this permission to desire.

Shields: Trump does understand desire. And he is or was very smart sometimes; he'll talk about how people want grandiosity and magnificence. It's the old William Randolph Hearst line that if the legend is better than the truth, print the legend. Don't say you're going to build a six-foot fence, ten yards by ten yards, to keep out a few rabbits on the border of El Paso. Say you're going to build a wall.

Jones: He would never socialize with the people in his base.

Shields: He has said as much. *Get those people away from me; they're losers*. And weirdly, they read that and keep coming back. That part I still don't totally understand, unless it's pure masochism.

Jones: Well, there are all sorts of people in the modern Western world who are intellectuals and who still go to Catholic or Anglo-Catholic churches to get the host so they can feel like, in Communion, they're getting the person of Jesus. That's at the heart of Christianity: through the breaking of the bread together, you commune with this person. And most of the Christians who go to Trump's rallies are anti-sacramental, so this is the new Communion for the Baptists and the Fundamentalists. They don't need the incense or the liturgy, or the Mass, or the art in the Gothic cathedral. Trump is their Communion. So you go there and you're receiving the body of Trump.

Shields: That ubiquitous red tie: the blood of the body of Christ.

Jones: And if you're a really traditionalist Catholic, you do these pilgrimages, and then you can say, *I was there*. For Trump's base, it's a spiritual pilgrimage: *I went to the rally*.

Shields: That does help explain why people weren't wearing masks at these rallies during the height of the pandemic. The moment you put on the mask, you're thinking with your rational self. When you take off the mask, you're obviously conveying fealty to the godhead. The reality is that when Trump got Covid, he had access to the best medical care in the world, and his base didn't/still doesn't.

Jones: That's an anti-Christ moment. When Jesus challenges conventional wisdom, it's always with the goal of liberation: *These religious leaders are pulling the wool over your eyes; Caesar's pulling the wool over your eyes; you're really free; you're really a subject, and you're a subject of mercy and compassion, and we can be on the journey together.*

Shields: When Trump challenges conventional science, it's, *Don't trust the science* (don't trust the things that have liberated humanity). And that's the religion. The religion is not believing in climate change.

Jones: Or the press.

Shields: That's the belief; the belief is in unbelief.

Jones: It's an attempt to be imperial. You want control over the press; you want control over religious institutions.

*

Shields: Trump is, to me, a bit like certain athletes, if one can say that, or other people who speak in entirely demotic language; it's never quite clear whether he's illiterate ("North Korea best not"; "very epic"; "very stable genius"; apropos structuring a season of *The Apprentice* around the opposition of a white team to a Black team: "Whether people like that idea or not, it is somewhat reflective of our very vicious world") or whether his malapropisms are (at least occasionally) an intentional form of modest witticism and/or faux populism, the key test case being, "I'm, like, a really smart person." The "like" here is near-genius.

*

Shields: One of the unique ways in which Trump talks is that he always listens to himself talking and is in active, perpetual, tragicomic dialogue/debate with what he's just said—his inability, in other words, to believe anything. (Montaigne: "We are, I know not how, double within ourselves, with the result that we do not believe what we believe and we cannot rid ourselves of what we condemn.") Told that he can't say X and do Y, he must say X and do Y; so, too, he has a need to articulate every thought he has ever had—

Shields: His commitment to self-immolation is unmissable and unending.

*

The message now is, "It's a fix." I've been able to message it.

*

Shields: The performer is always melancholy.

*

Shields: Fame is attention, and attention is love, and love can convert into hatred in an instant, because it's impossible to get enough love. (John Updike: "Celebrity is a mask that eats into the face.")

*

Ford Madox Ford: "We are all so afraid; we are all so alone; we all so need from the outside the assurance of our own worthiness to exist."

*

Pogo: "We have met the enemy and he is us."

*

Shields: When the president of the United States, during conceivably the most extreme crisis in the country shy of possibly the Civil War, stood in front of cameras and said, *Nobody likes me*, we understand that he has an open, manifestly bleeding, festering wound. He is obviously the opposite of Obama, who if anything was almost too dignified, too "classy," too sober, but Obama is closer to what we expect. The Trump presidency was just unusual. In a way, it's the Oprahfication of the country; everything finally comes down to Mommy and Daddy issues. My God, there's hardly an hour that goes by in which Trump does not issue a manifest cry for the intervention of a therapist. He is both plutocrat and utterly broken, mewling baby. He's so broken; the country is so broken.

You can only defeat a bully if you can understand what the bully's underlying psychology is. And I feel like I get Trump, because I've had to deal with a few bullies, as have we all, I suppose. And then as a personal essayist I'm very interested in finding that delicate balance between excavation and revelation, between "mirror and lamp." If I teach myself or my students anything, it's that you always have to wire everything through your own sensibility; that's what an essayist does. Trump takes that idea and politicizes it. His impulse is always to transgress the formal boundary, and he also understands that each of us (as one of eight billion people on the planet) views the world through our own particular, irreducibly subjective lens. He really gets that.

Jones: Seneca says, "Life is warfare." Trump knows that. He knows that we're primitive animals. People on the left can't see Trump as a human being because the left is moralizing, and it's weird that it becomes a virtue to be incapable of seeing someone as human.

He creates false homes, false fronts, like window dressings. It's Hollywood staging. But he also creates false homes for the people at the rallies—for a little while, you can get a false home. Because everybody's hurting, and the Trump rally is the substitute for psychotherapy.

The rally is, *I'm gonna own the libs, I'm gonna drink liberal tears from the cup of glory*. I've watched so many Trump rallies. I just think they're so entertaining.

Some people can't believe I would watch them. They ask how I can stand to watch, but when you watch a Trump rally, you're learning cultural theory. It's all there. I remember so clearly the way Trump was speaking one day: *They say they're the elites; I say we're the elites. Look at you, you're better looking, you're smarter, you're this, you're that.* Meanwhile, he's in some backwater airport somewhere.

C. S. Lewis has this great essay called "The Inner Ring" in *The Abolition of Man*. Lewis says all of humanity wants to be in the inner ring. And that's what QAnon gives you, right? *See, I'm in the inner ring now. Trump told me I'm in the inner ring.* And then when he's asked about QAnon—this is what I find great—Trump goes, *I don't know anything about QAnon, but I know they're against child molestation and abuse.* The fact that he can say that out loud and not be embarrassed is amazing.

Shields: I know what you mean. How does he do it? Maybe he's just a very good actor. Maybe he made it in Hollywood, after all—to bring us full circle. This might be the right moment to bring in this line from Ross McElwee, who's a documentary filmmaker I really love. Someone asked McElwee, What are the qualities that make a good documentary film subject? and he said, approximately, "Somebody who knows what his character is, is comfortable with his personality, and for dramatic purposes is willing to extend that personality." I think Trump ticks all three boxes. I'm not sure he knows who he is, actually, but he knows who his persona is, he's comfortable with it, and I think it's crucial that from 1982 (when he builds Trump Tower) to now, more than forty years later, you could almost chart the incremental expansion of his personality from just sort of a boring playboy pseudo-billionaire to a guy who plays a kind of autocrat on TV. He has just kept on amplifying his persona.

My hope remains that the very qualities that got him to the "top" will still conspire to unravel him. I do think he craves very deeply, in a way that's unspeakable, this unraveling of his performative self because, on some level, he wants to finally feel something authentic (so I believe)—to remove mask upon mask upon mask so he can actually feel something.

Jones: Amen.

About the Authors

David Shields is the internationally bestselling author of more than twenty books, including *Reality Hunger* (which *LitHub* named one of the 100 most important books of the last decade) and *The Thing About Life Is That One Day You'll Be Dead* (NYT bestseller). Shields wrote, produced, and directed *Lynch: A History*, a 2019 documentary about Marshawn Lynch's use of silence, echo, and mimicry as key tools of resistance. Shields's work has been translated into two dozen languages.

Scott Kent Jones is the former host and producer of the *Mockingbird* podcast and is now the host of *Give & Take* and the co-host, with Bill Borror, of *New Persuasive Words*. Jones, a Ph.D. candidate in Theology from Princeton Seminary, is an ordained minister.

www.ingramcontent.com/pod-product-compliance
Lightning Source LLC
Chambersburg PA
CBHW010329030426
42337CB00025B/4876